Halfling spring
an internet romance

JOANNE ARNOTT

Thompson-Nicola Regional District
Library System
300 - 465 VICTORIA STREET
KAMLOOPS, B.C. V2C 2A9

Halfling Spring© Joanne Arnott, 2013

PUBLISHED BY KEGEDONCE PRESS
11 Park Road
Neyaashiinigmiing, Ontario N0H 2T0
www.kegedonce.com
Administration Office/Book Orders
RR7 Owen Sound, ON N4K 6V5

Design: Red Willow Designs
and Ross Angus Design
Printed in Canada by Friesens Corp.

Library and Archives Canada Cataloguing in Publication

Arnott, Joanne, 1960-, author
    Halfling spring / Joanne Arnott ; illustrator, Leo Yerxa.

Poems.
ISBN 978-0-9868740-6-2 (pbk.)

    I. Yerxa, Leo, 1947-, illustrator II. Title.

PS8551.R773H34 2013   C811'.54   C2013-907889-4

Sales and Distribution - http://www.lpg.ca/LitDistco:
For Customer Service/Orders
Tel 1-800-591-6250 Fax 1-800-591-6251
100 Armstrong Ave. Georgetown, ON L7G 5S4
Email orders@litdistco.ca

We acknowledge the support of the Canada Council for the Arts which last year invested
$20.1 million in writing and publishing throughout Canada.

We would like to acknowledge funding support from the Ontario Arts Council, an agency
of the Government of Ontario.

table of contents

internet geographies
seeking alignment

i.   *riverspine (e-group one)*

there is a taste in the air
along the river some days

i really enjoy
how it draws my attention, tip

my head back—
where is this coming from?

what is the source of this
delicious flavour-scent?

where is it located?
what is it made of?

it's *teaandoranges*, i find out
casts this intriguing aroma

but what is *teaandoranges*?
i wonder

ii.   *the clock tower: big news*

specificallyjo is outrageously slow
delays along the way
make her later

teaandoranges is all efficiency, though
ready to dismiss the meet
and take to his feet

dadababy holds the space
within which the two can meet,
bringing their bodies along

for the first time

as similar to one another
as a catfish and a jaybird
an angel and an inuksuk

they sit on either side of the broker
and wish they were closer

iii.   *lightsinthenight (e-group two)*

teaandoranges opens his house
he leaves her the keys
and goes out

she putters around in dusty
back rooms, all full
of interesting papers

sometimes they meet
in the foyer

sometimes he teases her
in front of his friends

he makes her very nervous
and she really, really likes him,

a lot

iv.   *e-dating*

'well Alastair,' i write, 'i am afraid
i have developed quite a crush on you

it's beginning to have deleterious effects
in other areas'

you say, 'a sweet relationship
should not be clipped off,' &

'i would like to stay in touch'

well,
i do like touching, i think

i respond, 'the deleterious effects
have mostly evaporated'

i write love poems everyday,
i feed them to you

you feed me words & thoughts & images
feeling pools i can immerse myself in

rise up
refreshed

i develop cravings
for this food & drink

i love playing with you

savour

a mundane note draws
a warm smile of contentment
dragging my feet against response
to prolong contact
feeling such radiance

a lively discussion brings
the need to edit, oops
i think i used the word 'love' twice
how indiscreet

spy story

in telling the secret, there is release
& the danger of overspilling is less
just as joy follows thought
out of the opening made
diffuses across landscapes
unkind thoughts that flickered
along the edges of my strong, happy
visions, enchantments, now
move along into center stage

unflattering thoughts
pathetic
cruel words
haggle tooth

the buoyant possibilities have fled
without their food
& the bleak likelihoods
that are left
pull all along the frown lines, make
the face of my happiness obscure

waterglider

watergliders know the trick
is to step light, step wide
slip along the surface and
rest gently
across the top of things

but sometimes even watergliders
misstep, tumble, fall
an unexpected stride
into a deeper landscape

watergliders too will keen
sad echoes vibrate to the edge
of the rockbound pool
& turn back again

watermoccasin

because what i really want to do
is glide across the surface until
i find you, & devour you

capture that feeling of warm delight
& hold it within me forever

a kind of close close close
that will not destroy us

basking in the heat of you
& sliding along full-bellied

predatory desire awakens
from dreams of dry bites with
no venom

i am restless
rippling restless

wresting myself into place &
wriggling away again

desire wrestling desire wrestling desire

drink the sun

several roots by several routes
a constellation is struck, and
pleasure becomes his associate

the appreciation of one being
for another

the way the raindamp grasses turn
and drink the sun

water creatures

i.   *morphing*

water glider must exert one hundred times the force
of her own bodyweight
to re-break surface

where she swims with head aloft,
water moccasin
on a journey

her daughter calls to her
she calls and she calls and she calls

her voice leaping among the chorus
of the weeping grandmothers

her daughter calls to her
calls in a beckoning voice

her daughter slips through the pond
and, using her two human hands

pulls herself onto the rocky bank
and grins, saucy

flipping her tail at her mom

ii.   *accepting*

watching the water ripples
watching the grinning daughter

watching the sunlight on the surface of the pond
watching my own hands and breasts appear
above the waterline

swishing my tail in the depths until
all the remnants are stirred
from the bottom

such a beautiful day
such a happy time

beyond the grinning girl and the edge of the pond
she is sitting upon, so easily slipped

a place beyond the rocky edge
where angels and inuksuit tread

textuality

i write his name, Alastair
then i put a comma beside his name

Alastair,

i see that the comma beside his name
is like my hand on his shoulder, neck, face

i enjoy this
i write his name
i place my comma

Alastair,

climate change

i understand, this tragedy visited
by the greed of wealthy nations &
careless middle latitudes

upon northern folk who have their own
cherished ways, born upon the ice & snow
that is now disintegrating

who can recognize a land
so changed, & where will the people
base themselves, minds & hearts

the multiyear ice is in retreat
it is happening at an increasing rate
take a look around you

you know this is happening

i think of yin & yang
i think of the dao of civilizations
i think of the tiny dot of each in each

how to represent polarities
in a process of change, not the stasis
of oppositional natures

but the fluidity of waves

imagine, though, that is what i'm doing
because my nerves are rattled & i
have to do something

imagine what might be revealed through
this process of change, the human resilience
called up in the face of such massive

worldshifting

an attitude of curiosity, too, is not inappropriate
is it travesty to gaze at tragedy with clear eyes?

imagine that the icefields of the world
are a suit of clothes
the earth has lived in long on long, and
all of the animals, cultures, people who know
the ice as solid home
are about to be shirked

some care more for the populous regions
for the storming & flooding of those greedy nations
& careless industrialized communities
some care more
for all the one by one by one
human experiences

all of the innocents of all of the nations
sharing hearts & one single planetary base

earth is a goddess who may change
her clothes, may shift about any time she chooses
we must all be alert to gather ourselves
quick as we can to the safest place
until she has quieted, comfortably settled, once again

do i know this, or do i imagine this, or
do i believe this?
yes, all of the above

the ice as it leaves incrementally
may bring gifts of revelation
the perfect & whole body of a mammoth
one mammoth, maybe two,
who have been long buried

a southern wind, effect of global warming,
arriving with enough love to blow
the soul back into these animals

the world
is tipped on its axis

ancient animals imagined
rising from long sleeping & all
those moribund years

standing
vulnerable at first
then with increasing certainty

to gaze back at the world
with those miraculous eyes

inuksuit & angels

whatever you have seen, can i
taste it on your skin if i
ever come close enough to
close in with my faulty mouth? not
a guaranteed thing

i listen to the surviving twins'
boisterous takes on love & immigration
i pull something from myself
by blasting love songs and balancing
elementary schools with academic
papers

i draw a fragile flower of self
& give it to a glossy magazine, wondering
where this, where this, where i ask you
will this take me?

to moor against you is a pleasure but
how guilty a pleasure is it?
unknown

beer, wine
inuksuk, dream catcher

everything has a source

i like a man with clarity, but
do fear a harsh aspect
& running up against clear
disapprobation

piles of rock that are treasures to men
& arguments about the accuracy
of angel imagery
marker and messenger and guide
visible & imagined

what is the most beautiful thing
god created?
angels, men, caribou
or woman in her web of relations

a cure for longevity (a taste of honey)

i received an email missive
the author asserted
that a daily dose

of cinnamon & honey
would cure many ailments
including 'longevity'

i sat with this information
talked it over with friends

was this just a poor choice of words
or a statement of the facts, deeply cynical?

cancers
diabetes
AIDS

hangover
hunger
huntington's

dead twins
unhappy marriages
community demands

longevity

i eat cinnamon daily
but honey i avoid, too painful

playing catch with Alastair:

i lean way back
i pull my heart out
i throw it, just as far as i can

simple happiness

there is someone in this world
that my hands are interested
in gently running across
in smoothing
in touching
in stroking
in getting to know

my hands have spoken
my hands have let somebody know
and liked the answers they received, now
stored in my bones

my hands are happy
moving lightly across the tasks
that fall to them

my hands have shaped a poem
to celebrate this
simple happiness

flight risk

he said he would like
to trade

she spread out her shawl on the ground
began pulling out her handmade trinkets
laying them out one by one

she felt a shadow
crossing the sun

without looking up, hastily,
she began to gather her things

wings stirring, body
already rising

stopping places (Victoria)

chickadee & sparrow
are feasting around me
the elders move slow while
the young are quick with chatter

tender relationships
you tell me, should not be
clipped

i watch the restless harbour
through the delicate pink of
new cherry blossoms

think of you, think of snow
as the cars go, people walk
seaplanes rev, ferries find
their journeys' end

every day, every moment
of every day is an opportunity
to say, this
is my stopping place

i thank you for all of your gifts
my path turns here

like the air that cossets the world
like the sea that laps against
all the islands of the world
i find no stopping place

only the slow beckoning touch
like the long rays of an afternoon's sun

seasonal

in new light of spring
earth sends a song
up through roots of
winter trees

trees dance
earth energies begin to spill
from one hundred thousand
fingertips

laughter rises
laughter rises
through bellies of trees
radiates outward
linking forest in
camaraderie

as sun sets
small, tender light
of evening is seen

trees settle into chant
and will continue, night and day,
until deep heat
of summer
is here

new love

if i were to carve it, would i choose
stone, bone, wood, or animal horn
how would i characterize this
how would i animate it
what story will i tell
what story will our children tell
what story will our children's children tell

if i were to weave it, would i choose
birch, cedar, porcupine quill, hair of goat or dog
how would i represent this
how would i express it
what song will i sing
what song will our children sing
what song will our children's children sing?

i wonder what gifts can be gathered
what gifts my family can gather
loading the boat with gifts
to buy me back from my groom and
leave him sated

i wonder who will steer the boat
i wonder how long the sea journey

allowing me to return
to my true home and my
new love

divesting (moon)

after investing comes
divesting

i want to flee the fullness of my own want
i want to flee the tension of possible futures
i want the wave function to simply collapse
into a realm of the given, & simplicity

it is true, i am implacable
it is true, i am patient, flexible
it is true, i am exceedingly tiny & small
about to disappear again under a leaf

after appearing comes
disappearing
naturally

weather or not (you love me)

on a day when
cherry blossoms
are obscured
by buoyancy
of snowfall

my mind clears
my song spills
my body rejoices
in certainty & in clarity

east

becomes the promised land
where sun rises & all
forms of happiness

release from primordial urge
through human form, and
through awkward moments

that pass as each moment
will, and from little seeds
in the ground that break

spill
rise up
green & willing

how it feels (arrow's wake)

this conversation
is beginning to feel

less like a conversation
more like a journey

married or not
whether or not (you love me)
ready or not

i am the arrow
aimed & released &
shooting true

does the arrow
stop in the heart, or
carry on through?

if stopped, does it make
a sweet home there, or
must it be plucked?
plucked & tossed?

if, in preparing to receive
the heart stands open so wide
the arrow passes clean through

who or what emerges
from you?

woman in flight becomes arrow
arrow through heart becomes love

heart renovated through passage
arrow transformed through heart

how it feels is not
stick with fashioned tip
& well-placed feathers

though the motion is the same
focus, sure aim, smooth passage
swift & true

how it feels is sure body
fluttering mind, & a desire
to see much more clearly

a patience with both
my own disturbances, &
those of the man

i am flowing to

delving

i.

some things are negotiable, we find
some things simply are not
holding hands is negotiable
for instance, whereas
walking is not

holding hands is negotiable
for a lot of reasons, i know
some people are very particular
about where they place their hands
and how comfortable or uncomfortable
attempting to pace oneself, alongside
another self, might be—i wouldn't
want to throw off
your stride, or
disorient you unduly

holding hands is definitely
negotiable
(i have pockets)

ii.

i have pockets
lots of pockets
some hidden, some not
i have pockets i am willing
to give and take resources from
i have pockets i am only
willing to turn out
with a friend

some of my pockets are deep
no end of delving these
you may dive in, swim
for days or years
crawl to the rim for release
spooked, or sated

some pockets hold mystery
they are portals
to ancient places
some of these require sacrifice
some of these will draw you in
against your will

i see that, whether or not
you would like to hold hands
you would like to see into
these pockets
you would like to slip your fingertips
along the edges of these pockets
of mine
to test the texture and relative heat
to sample the scent, perhaps, on the
edges of things

i see that, whether or not
you would like to hold hands
you are hungry for me
you are full of thirst
you are alone in some precise way
that only a visit
all along the edges of my pockets
can cure

iii.

i am like a ball pitched
by a bored god

pulled from a ragged
pocket, and tossed

i find myself travelling
with purpose, at speed

unerring and true
i am aimed at you

i
am

hungry
for the taste, the

shine of you, i
am thirsty for

the depths of the pools
the sea-salt waters

of you, i am
more

like a hungry infant bird
than a grown woman, yet,

i am more
like a grown-up woman
than a ball

of any sort at all

iv.

when i was a girl
i adored the mystery
of my grandmother's sweater pockets

sometimes, she would allow me
to dip my little girl hands in
to explore

sometimes, i had to ask

sometimes, i would find chiclets
or a roll of mints
small change, crumpled tissues

even an empty pocket
was a space to investigate and, at
the very least

held affection for me

v.

walking
might be negotiable

after all

delicious

i would like to show you
the cherry blossomed tree, and
i would like to walk through snowfall

with you, too. i would like to
look with you, listen with you, guess
at the scents on the wind

with you, find out the why of you
through all the human means
at our disposal. furthermore

i would like you to learn me
thoroughly, too. i would like to taste
those things you perceive as

delicious

i would like to taste
just like that
to you

aspects

the other side of springtime
is death, when the snow melts
the bodies of winter & all
lost objects
are revealed

cherry blossoms festoon
not just trees, but funerary urns
all of us seem to be called
to dance with our ghosts
to lay them down gently

if we can

luminosity has settled upon us
the long, low calls we are responding to
these are not inventions
these are things of the air & the sea & the season
i take my life in both my hands: i want you

we can turn out our pockets slowly
we can let the coins fall without clutching
we can make new stories out of old ones, &
out of all of the sweetness of life, tasted
again, or tasted for the first time

wholesome

affection most feline
rubbing up against
the edges of things

immersion in some intrigue
in the form of person as text
following themes & motifs

with a more than passing interest
flipping pages but slowly, pretty much
absorbed

in these wholesome activities

pod

i say, Alastair, the boat
is both small & big
big enough to lay down together
paddles drawn in, drifting
small enough to be toppled
in a quick spring storm
however hard both paddlers work
to right the craft
to save
the journey

& then i forget
& then i tell you, i'm sorry
i didn't have time to write
a love poem for you today

i say, we are in the same boat
& you seem to agree, nous sommes, & yet

the pod is neither peagreen boat
nor safe haven, only

an imagined craft that rhymes with god
& holds nothing, or perhaps, holds everything

an imagined craft that is woven of
the full spectrum of light, & of dreams

patience
temperance
virtue

my uncle, the one who steals pens
tells me he loves me

that must be enough
for now

crow sex i

on a morning grey, crow calls
in that specific voice she sometimes uses

crow or cat or crow
i look to see

there on the sidewalk across the street
crow is fucking crow

i listen to her feline calls
watch as her crowfriend dismounts

alone on the porch in the suburb
what is all this to me

crow sex ii

clouds part & the sun bathes
the street again, i hear her
just one low crow moan

midway up the evergreen
my side of the street this time
the rendezvous

a third crow descends
landing with a thump
on the crowlovers backs

the three stand along the limb
the new arrival standing vigil

the crowlovers apart, but
connected

the three stand along the limb
she shows her chosen one

a little tenderness

like attracts like (opposites attract)

if i were an old woman
reaching out reflexively

to keep my balance
& if you were there

you would do then
what you have done here

but i am not an elder yet
& even then, i may want more

than what can be given
in the shock of the moment

in a spirit of gallantry
& without

disturbing your self

i sit among peonies
i wear the cloak you made for me

i listen for the sound of your
deep speaking

i drink the tenderness
you send most willingly

what do you like, though
i wonder

what do you like
what do you want, Alastair?

weaning (fear of haemorrhage)

maybe i broke it
this beautiful delicate
craft i was building
with you

maybe i read you wrong
maybe i heard you wrong
maybe i mistook you
maybe i didn't trust enough

a wave of unhappy emotion arrives
without letter or text: so porous am i

or perhaps, so divided
i cannot distinguish

whether this is yours or mine, this
crumpling of the heart

grieving that lodges
midbreast

i wish i knew better
i wish i knew you better

i wish i felt better
i wish i felt closer to you

maybe i broke it though
out of fear, out of anger

maybe that's the only chance
i get

a taste of honey (the shadow of death)
with thanks to the author of Psalm 23

i am going into shock
at my own behaviour
i cannot believe that i
thought that this was
the right thing to do

The Lord is my shepherd; I shall not want.

i sat with my grandmother
in the hours leading up to
her death, & that was my
fortune, to be her handmaiden
not death's handmaiden

*He maketh me to lie down in green pastures: he leadeth
me beside the still waters.*

i walked for a week with
a man who meant me harm
& i found a way to get help—
that was my fortune,
to be released from harm

*He restoreth my soul: he leadeth me in the paths of
righteousness for his name's sake.*

i am so full of grief
my body did not agree to
this course of action
perhaps i was angry
to slap my own needs aside

*Yea, though I walk through the valley of the shadow of
death, I will fear no evil:*

perhaps it was only fear
a trickster i know
from a long time ago
i can't say i am glad you are
free of me

*for thou art with me; thy rod and thy staff they comfort
me.*

i can only hope you see past
my pride, or feel strong enough
to answer the unanswered questions
maybe you get the rhythm already
of these approaches & flights

*Thou preparest a table before me in the presence of mine
enemies:*

i can only pray for guidance
divine intervention of some sort
a mercy killing, or perhaps
a mercy fuck: better yet,
a hand at my pillow

thou anointest my head with oil; my cup runneth over.

Alastair,
i say

i hope this makes you feel at least a teeny bit better
you write

& really,
it does

hand to hand (surrender)

if i put
everything
the all of you
and the all of me

into the hands of the grandmothers
into the hands of the grandfathers

then
i must
release
all of us, as well

and i have surrendered
all of these
small human
entanglements

letting go
is difficult
where river holds land
to the sea

i drift along
a sunlit day
head to toe
longing

Lightsinthenight

Moving right along from thoughts
of orca feeding down the food chain
to aboriginal dancers moving the crowd
with superman & zorba
to the mass graves of Canada
out of the local news, finally
gone international

i was standing in the back field
watching the green folds of light
draped across the sky, thinking
of the hems of the robes of
the priests and the nuns
wondering about divinity
universe of mystery

sometimes the questions flock
far beyond the reaches of our ability
to make answers

sometimes just sharing the questions
sometimes just making the reach
not alone this time, but
in company

sometimes the past and present fold
and i am lost somewhere between
a cold back field gazing through starlight
and a small book in a small shop
somewhere
i have never been

sometimes the headlines arrive
leaving skid marks across the heart

game of risk

Alastair, when i try to work, desire
calls me in a low crowmoan, distracting
i am always turning to you
i am always turning to you, both
where i hold you
where your words have touched and captured
entire realms of me
and through the world outward
where your words come again
and capture me more
i am wholly interested
i am dreaming you in the daytime
i am climbing over myself
i am tremblingly full

Alastair,
when i try to work
desire calls through me
in a low crowmoan
like a river in the rush of spring's
earthquenching overflow
i am reaching out in every direction
watery hands quicken across the land
watery hands quicken in a fretful search
i am willing to pour myself over you
i am willing to pour myself out
i need to hold you in this world
i need to find you and hold you
i need to find you and hold you in this world, Alastair

Baanaabe kwe!

Baanaabe kwe! they say
she was most beautiful
and he enjoyed her
sensual attentions, and
she did set him free

Baanaabe kwe! they say
the two met upon the shore
a year later, he of the land
she of the inland sea
& their tender, newly born

halfling

Strong Wind

we had rain last night
it was cold
large wet flakes of snow
settled on the playground

today the sun is shining
the playground is quiet
but for the footsteps
of a person unseen
planes overhead
cars on a nearby street
all travelling

you are my Strong Wind
revealing yourself to me
as a gift made in exchange
for frank honesty

i see now what your bow
is strung with

i see now what you use
to pull your sled

no more
guesswork

how a burnt-faced girl can win
such a dazzling friend as this

defies all logic
and still, supports the ethics of

be true
you say you want to drive your sled
under the shimmering lights of night

i long for this, too, i will
this journey

witness to the miracles you have harnessed
& the handcrafting of your sled & harness, too

deeply horn

these are the things i dream of

standing nearby
such a powerful taste to the energies
of two beings

two beings in proximity
i have been dreaming that one for months
it may never leave me

watching for signs
sensing the air for messages
looking

indirectly, peripherally
increasing the gaze
following elemental flows

more than one gaze, joining
all that can be stated & spoken
through the eyes

with & without my reading glasses

listening for the sounds
that all of human nature
can make

allowing the strange drifts to
come & go, extraordinary vessels carrying
extraordinary flows

Can I touch, smell, see, feel her?

touching
feeling a touch
feeling a near touch, also

hoping to verify the ghosted songs
with sensual evidences of human
presence, a scent, a taste

how many legs has she, if any
& are they made of stone or flesh?
are both legs mortal, & was she born with them?

& is he the sort of lover
that disappears in the light of a candle?
has he strung his bow with the milky way?

does he draw his sled with a rainbow?

i am as shy as burnt offerings
the leaves of the aspen tremble
the bag of gifts is set upon the ground

a horn of plenty, deeply
more deeply, Alastair,
more

Can I touch, smell, see, feel him?

placing my commas upon you
prodding your joints for signs of
piled rock behaviour

palming my hands across your shaved head
palpating your shoulder blades for evidence
touching your eyelids & lips

hearing your breath
sensing your breath
scenting

when you are asleep
i will be checking all around the beach
with a small sprig of fire

for shed bird
or animal bodies
to hide from you

these are my dreams

stories in the morning (eagle)
with thanks to Dobie Gray, "Drift Away"

i.
for a time i could sit
in the midst of a busy household
& talk story with you
late into night
&, when so far away
the sun would rise
& you would open your eyes
a row of stories sat waiting
having flown to you in the night
arriving untired from my hands

now, though, i am in retreat
from my household
i sit on a cherry stump outside
or i lay across my bed
with the radio on
i am trying to absorb, release,
balance, make harmony with
all of the songs & stories
held so long, or held
just for a little while

& there is a song i could use
to write my autobiography, how
these stanzas represent the world
i was going out into for the first time
& why i was called to learn every word
& all of the places & times the song
provided a way through for me
i could make a passing peace with the world
through listening, through singing
with my whole heart

& these later stanzas, how they all curl around
how i feel about you now
what significance you have for me
even so far away as this
even without stories in the morning
or any words at all, sometimes
now that the world is better known
much better understood, less confusing
to me personally & it seems, no more
predictable, for all that

if i were, myself, a story
i could fly to you through the night
& arrive untired

ii.
one story we tell is of a falcon
bonded with a human
& the bird, though predatory, begs

for a glove
to rest upon
sometimes

the falconer responds, he will
hold his hand aloft
in many places

at many times
without hesitation
with enthusiasm

promising food &
soothing touch
across her feathers

the story transforms
with the words
'I shall come'

the idea of me
calling for you
& you, flying forth

iii.
when you fly to me
i am not a bird any more
i am a woman once more

laying under an open sky
a huge expanse of land around me
wide earth upholding me

no danger & no need for
predatory wiles of any kind

listening to the beat
of your wings, sounding
wingbeats across many miles

i can hear you

like a pulse of the world
like a close up heartbeat
like a ceremonial drum

both steady & strong

waxing moon (shine upon me)

a full blossom sunset
is followed by a rising
waxing moon

we give & take our food
in small parcels

& savour

i awaken with radiance
spilling from my heart region

how steadily it grows

after moonset
a glorious sunrise:
shine upon me

uses of the erotic (the erotic as power)
with thanks to Audre Lourde

I.
the magician strides into the clearing
she stamps her foot, thrice, she shakes
her rattle
she alarms you with the power that
she has harnessed through her gaze
you turn your eyes to your task
you pretend
you didn't notice her arrival
as your blood heats and
your breath comes quick
as she calls you out with her
sly chants and unusual
rhythmic dance
hold your ground
hold your ground
keep your eyes averted
she is all about you now and you
will never be the same
after this

II.
the star is a healing dancer too
with water she slakes every thirst
even those you never knew
you had

she washes you gently from head to toe
all of the back of you
all of the front of you
all of the inside of you
all of the land nearby

she takes out your heart
she takes out your brain
she bathes them tenderly
she asks, do you want these back?

you say yes to the brain
about the heart, you are unsure

chanticleer dreams

waking with a thump
from a dream, almost
topple from my roost

when chanticleer woke
from this same dream
his favoured wife

called him a fool
for believing in dreams—
murder will out! he argued

later, mollified, watching
a butterfly, he walked
straight into danger

in his own side yard

halfling bear (eclipse)

the trophy hunter has it
the scientists & the media
celebrate, debate, discuss
photos of the corpse fly
all around the world
& linger for years

the miracle of courtship
alignment sought & found
the passing of a honeymoon
the wonder of apparent difference
transcended with pleasure

the private rendezvous of
polar bear & grizzly, followed
by months of solitary gestation
of nurturing, nursing
feeding
teaching the young

all the years of a young bear's life
discoveries, missteps, accomplishments
the cultural patterning inhabited, as
taught by the mother
& the world met, step by step

all these
disappear

into bloodlust & big money
dna proofs & a too small sample
the death of a halfling bear reveals
the minds of scientific observers
& all forms of prejudice: miscegenation
still, so scandalous

this is not a freakshow
but evidence of life unfolding
& showing its shape as it goes
the elders say, *usually they fight*
but not this time

inuksuit tales

inuksuit observations &
archival photographs altered

i.   *urban inuksuit*

worries about change
worries about shifts
in our world base

species adrift, flora &
fauna, all of us shifting
boundaries, gone

wandering, showing up
in unexpected places
four seasons do just what

they feel like, instead of
what they have always
been observed to do

inuksuit surging
far further to the south
than they have ever been

seen before, in urban areas
all along the 49th parallel
gazing offshore

urban inuksuit reports
from the west coast: she
is sighing over salt water

at english bay, birthing
many tiny images & fist-
sized inuksuit (also observed)

urban inuksuit report
from the great lakes: he
is befriending bicycles

she is stepping offshore
crossing the great waters
on an inward journey

ii.   *inuksuk 1924 (first photo)*

this one is me, recognize
the way i hold my body
just so

with the dog expressing
an interest, i reach out
i touch

when the wind comes up
& i am hatched
i am still cognizant

of the snow
of the sky
of the hint

of the dog
beside me

iii.   *inuksuit (second photo)*

well-spaced
well balanced
well matched

gazing together
at the focal point
& a wide horizon

cross-hatching occurs
& all become
hints of themselves

mere suggestions
brighten sunlight while
silence strengthens shadow

dreaminess takes the whole
landscape
& us, too

iv.   *safe place to make camp (final photo)*

a very small image
& if we try to make
it bigger

than it is
it becomes
less beautiful

very small is very good
as you can see
plenty

of scope
& a wonder-
filled view

the name
for this one
is true

hatching
cross-hatching
together

a softer, fuller
treatment

water walk

the part of the dream i failed to tell
because i couldn't place it yet
i have now placed: the road scene.
i pull up in a car, the driver says,
"here?" I say, "yes, that's his place."

I look at your fine house and the
coach house office beside it, more fine
than anything you might have
dreamt up for yourself. i have
the small black disc in hand

and i leave the car. i do not cross
the street to your house and office
but head off the other way
at a good pace. I have my adventures
i succeed in retrieving your message

at the last.

The part of the dream i like best
is the walk i take out of the cavern
my small son on my hip, i am
slow walking through cool waters

i dream these water dreams
each time i am ready
to give birth. they
reassure.

The little coach house i know
is the place you practice
your doctoring, a place
of affection for me, a place
of passion

love doc
word doc
dream talk
water walk

a taste of wonder

it seems odd to cling to this
as compelling truth, it seems
foolish & insubstantial, seems
unsteady & unwise

yet when i look for relief
from distress, i consider you
when i cast about for a taste
of wonder

i just centre on the well
& draw up the blossoming trees
with heady springtime aromas
i draw up the hazy image

of you, & birds fly forth
i draw up the deep taste of
right from my passionate core
& i know, whether or not

it's going to be alright,
it is alright, just now

poem-centric

it may not be perverse
but it is certainly inverse
& perhaps obverse, as well

any poem-centric relationship
is bound to be verse
of some kind

lap

from my mother's womb & down past
her knees & ankles on a metal bed
eventually returned to her, startled

& swaddled
i spent as many hours as i could
on the lap of my mother

my father
my grandmother
my grandfather

my four elder sisters
my aunts, uncles, cousins
anybody big enough, i'd guess

hearing stories, singing songs
or just listening to the things
people say, while cuddling

a small child

then the search for other sorts of laps
big enough to curl up on, some called
my lover, some, my community

the other forms of lap all mingle and merge
with this primordial experience of love
the way a dog will slake his thirst

the way the ocean intimately visits
all the shores in the world, and the clear
waters delicately curl across all of the lands

in myriad forms: the small creek,
the slough, the mighty river, the pond,
the lake, the humble mud puddle, the inland sea

lap is associated with aprons
lap is a patch, or passing this way again
lap is about receiving, too, gracefully

whether my lap is one of mermaid
green or granite grey or pale brown skin
it is a generous place, as small children

know, & others
might attest
if need be

Love.

I.   *transition between worlds*

If i can pull Alastair from my chest
and allow him to stand in a room
that I am also standing in, that will be
good. If I can pull the optimistic trees
from my womb and allow them to grow free
in the world outside of me, that, too, will
be good. If I can pull Alastair's hand and
clasp it in my own, and walk with him
between the trees in real time, that will
be heaven. If I canpull Alastair's arms
around me, there among the laughing
trees, that will be magic. If I can pull
Alastair's heart and mind, spirit and
body, over me like a net and rest inside
of him, then i will be his, he will be mine:
love, followed by a full stop.

II.   *preparations for the real*

If I can see Alastair across a room and
watch him stand and move and hear his
voice in real time, that will be good. If
I can come close enough to taste Alastair,
that too will be good. If I can receive a
touch, from Alastair, if I can give and
receive a flock ofmigrating touches to
and from Alastair, thatwill be heaven. If
I can receive Alastair deeply, deeply
within my self, that will be magic. If the
words and the silences, the rhythms and
the rest points, the lust and the longing,
the romantic minds and the daily minds,

cohere and form a net with us inside,
then I will be his, and he will be mine:
love, followed by a full stop.

access

while others enjoy
their voyages, i am
impatient, and i
must wait

my desire
i must hold
& sit quietly with

it is a good companion

immersion

i want to go on a walking journey
& explore you at a slow pace

i want to listen as stories fall

i want to catch stories & toss them
back & forth as we walk along

i want to swim the length of you

i want to fly from one hand to the other
& back again

wind's up

wind's up in the suburb
petals buoyantly descending

pink overtakes the lawns &
the gutters

a child grabs a handful
like a snowball

a woman kicks along through
as if scattering
silent autumn leaves

wind carries us

hair flying
blossoms tossing

petals race me
all along the sidewalk

carrion

that pop culture image of surrender
the available woman lolling about in
an open landscape

my own disparaging response to an image
of peace and surrender, & how the two
merge

i glimpse a self who is free of the need
for predatory wiles, and free
of danger

then i jerk back, burnt, sneering
at my own vision
looks like carrion

while part of me flows toward a rendezvous
i am dragging along a sputtering bar wench self
who never sleeps

armed to the teeth, she may always sneer
at the carrion women lolling about the world, waiting
to be eaten

she may rise up at unexpected moments
and hiss

all i can tell you is
she too can be seduced
(she likes wrestling)

cherry blossom sacrifice (Ottawa)

petals impulsively scooped
from the tarmac, shoved
into pockets

transported thousands of miles
to subside, a small browning pile
at bedside

regardez

water steadily slipping through
the wood of the closed lock, the sound
as soothing as any other sound
in the world

if the heart
stands open
gathering nuance &
letting it flow

another idea is free to slide in
with the solidity of a train
pulling cattle cars
filled with the fear

of trapped people
doomed to life & death
all of us in our bodies &
no hope of tearing free

water in overflow
cascading from the top of the
locked gate, gravity assists
in making a balance

conceptual walls like
in a public place, or
over a lunch date
demand some redirection

& so sorrow settles in
i drop food on its head
conversation slides
across the top, a pair

of water gliders

knowing the depth is there
we make little vortexes
with our feet, & keep moving

when the water level drops
and the lock is exposed

i feel afraid, i move to the edge
of the walkway, face averted

stealing anxious glances
at the long fall beside me

this is how i learn
how much i trust the water

urban bark

on Elgin I pause for the traffic light
my eye drawn by a host of rusted staples
on the pole beside me

I reach out and stroke my hand across
time-softened metal, so populous
a stiff fur of deep brown

so many events have come and gone
so many announcements made, good times
predicted, posters layered

lights change, I move on
part of an agile human flow
I glance back at the pole

and along the street at the others
this one, the one that I touched
has hand and foot holds secured

to either side, metal grips planted
all the way to the top

metal limbs and urban bark
this scarred tree, culturally modified
in the extreme

made to a human scale, meant
to be scaled by a human
perhaps me

effigies

scraps and fragments
capture the moments

bells chime
the quarter hour

can be used to build
something long and strong

beetle glitters
copper, small

like you
on another day

cherry scented
courtyard, sunlit

after the parting
of the ways

hair falls
over my face

you are a palm-sized stone
i curl my fingers around

cascade of morning glories
down the broken fence

the high meadow

i am a door you have opened
a passage you have entered
i am a changing landscape
under your hand

for now, i can drink you down
imbibe you at molecular levels
let you all the way in
to my full self

i cannot think beyond this
i cannot see beyond this place
i cannot feel any more than the
alchemy blend

i feel a fear of change
from one shape to another, the
formless center place of between—
no solidity, no definition

vulnerable to a cocoon
that may, at any moment, become
bored, distracted, feel a shift
in priorities, and

peeling himself too easily off
become some fine winged thing
oblivious to
my de-structuring

bee and hummingbird cover
the high meadow
a too vulnerable life stalls
on a grassy blade

enthusiasm

sunset ottawa
i think of you
clouds pass over
the river and
the highway too

planning a reprise
visit with you
already i am

bright gold disc
in silvery heavens
dazzling display
at the end of each day
i think of you

touch of long rays
swift shifting hues
qualities of light
and of waters too

already i am

and should the stars
and all the constellations choose
to shine forth and burn through
the cloud mansions that stand
between me and you

and i can fly true, arriving
just beside you

will you say, not yet
                not yet
                    not yet

or will you say, already
                    i am

rattlesnake (Winnipeg)

walking along on
human feet, he sees
a rattler and, stepping
beyond,
more and more rattlers
marking the path
larger and larger
stepping more and
more slowly
fear builds

do not disturb
do not disturb

beyond fear lies
the sloughing of the skin
slipping away from the old
with a shiny
new presentation
skin
so tender
colours well-defined
excellent grip and release
of a tactile nature, moving
along

shake of the tale, rattler
a warning
a song that sounds so sweet

rattler swallows the source
becomes that forever loop
of eternity

little news (Vancouver)

the trolley bus makes a fast curve through
intersecting streets, eastbound on Broadway
then northbound on Granville, executing the turn
without detaching pole from wire

a man stops beside my table, sets down his bag
insists upon discussing with me the changeable
weather: one coat he removes, another he pulls
from the bag & fusses slowly into

the sun is hot on my legs and the shade
is cool on my head and hands: what more
can i tell you? there is little news, but this:
we are like a catfish & a water glider

breathing different elements
nearby, a water lily is thriving
rooted below me
flowering above you

twofold

all the slow detail
of my ordinary life

split up the middle
by the wild, lush growth

of this
new thing

all of my inside
all of my soft gut

coming alive at the sound
of your voice and humming

joy when i allow myself
to focus on future plans

when i tell myself
i must be reasonable

attend to the important work
of my present day life

maintain
and nourish

love becomes an ache
in my belly, scented

with sorrow

when i am with you
i am contented
i am exactly where i want
to be, i am
deeply patient

we fold together and
move apart with ease

home has become thus
divided for me

inside my own life, this
renegade passion pulls me
aside and holds me midair

how the pieces can be made
to fit and function together
is not clear

i balance in a twofold life
strained by duality
doing nothing very well

and everything
as best i can

joanne & alastair

exhausting herself with an
ambitious plan, so far she has flown
from the flowers
her food

so fast has she flown
her small body consumed
all stored resources, and
a little bit more

faltering
faltering
fluttering her speedwings

becoming desperate
over the wide
water passage

stepping through the three worlds
in which he is at home, crane feels
the small body drop
upon his breast

there, there, hummingbird
shh shh

he learned about beauty and
sensual love

while running his fingertips gently
through the plumage of an owl

for her, the lessons came up
through the thick undercoat

of a rabbit, pale grey, and the longer
brown-black tips of its mammal hair

while she lays across the path
proposing marriage
to a feral rabbit

he has taken to flying, flying, flying
through the air

mortality and immortality
intertwining on a beach

the sacred is palpable

it rises from the ground
and through our fingertips

it arrives in waves and moves
with tidal grace

lifting a song
using the voices of waters

and the slow flux of rocks
and mountains

we are the small flowers of the morning
we are the creatures of the earth and

of the stars

Bird Companions

As I lie here hour after hour, I seem to enter
the wild pastimes of the cliff, and to become
a companion of the cormorants and crows.

> --J.M. Synge, "The Aran Islands"

i.   *fish*

heron stepping long-legged & slow
along the shoreline
sharp-eyed observer of all that flows
below the river surface

a quick darting response, immersing
your head to claim
this fish's life
for your own

then, head aloft again
you strike a calm, calm & stately, pose

becoming airborne
is always a challenge, with those
broad blue wings & fine walking limbs
& graceful neck

to organize everything
& launch skyward
is difficult, yet daily you accomplish
the task

you do fly with poise & strength
& build a sturdy nest among the trees

ii.   *delta*

river winds across land
gathering clay & soil & seed
building a delta that opens wide
a lush expanse
where red-winged blackbird stays
to sing
all year

the geese & duck arrive
& they leave
arrive
& they leave
return
& then they leave again

season follows season
year after year they make their path
of wide world migrations

& they do stop by me
they do
to rest & feed
but only for a little while

iii.   *fish*

struck by heron's bill
& caught

lifted dripping from my home
into the sky i go

will i be swallowed?
will i slide all the way along

the inside of that neck
come to rest

deep within
become one

with the heron?
or will i topple to the side

fall from a high place
torn?

iv.   *delta*

a wide orchestral interplay
of water & wild flower
mud & tough, tall grass
the songs of the birds & the frogs
liven our hearts

creation story (Iqaluit)

old bones in the backfield
scapula in dust, shards
of pelvis

lifted, dusted, brushed
reassembled into a perfect-pitched
vessel

lifting the old woman parts
dreaming the flesh into place
and the bighead babies

passing through again
tongue probing
broken teeth

in a mouth warm
with saliva
breath

whistling through
whistle shaved from fibula
knuckles

dance
in my hand
remaking the self

from the vitality of the field
from minerals and wind
from starlight sunlight moonshine

weaving the eons forward and back
moulding the lichen and moss into
rockpiled mountains

the boney pleasure of a long hike
around the bay, and the deep cold water
penetrating the flesh of each leg

assembled well enough to carry
a leather boot in each hand
walk barefoot with me through

the long afternoon, through
the tidal shifting day, through
the sleep-tossed night, boots

left by the door of the house, bones
deeply embedded in the soft turns
of your flesh, ribs lightly

dancing the rhythms of sleep
dreams unfurling on the inside while dawn
is slipping in i have this night, this night

basking in the warmth of your sleepheat
stirring against you and curling toward you
and breathing in the deep shelter of your arms

Acknowledgements

My thanks to Leo Yerxa for receiving a mountain of poems, and sifting through to create a smaller flock of images that ground, suggest, reflect, and amplify the core concerns of the collection. It is an honour and a pleasure to travel with you, in this book.

Some of these poems (or versions of these poems) previously appeared in: *W'daub Awae: Speaking True* (Kegedonce Press, 2010), *xxx ndn: love & lust in ndn country* (Aboriginal Writers Collective of Manitoba, 2011), *the family of crow* (chapbook, leaf press, 2012), and/or in these journals: *Contemporary Verse 2, Event, Exile Quarterly, Rampike, sub-Terrain, Weatherbell no. 2* (occasional), and *poemimage* (online illustrated poetry journal).

The pile of poems would not have found the way to polished manuscripts if it were not for the substantial assistance of The Woodcock Fund, The Writers Trust of Canada. I also acknowledge the support of BC Arts Council and Canada Council for the Arts, for support in the form of writing time on a spectrum of projects. My thanks to Barbara Kuhne, Kateri Akiwenzie-Damm, and Jamie Reid for feedback on various stages of this manuscript. Many of the poems were shared among friends on online groups: many thanks to the e-webs of poetic playmates.

This collection originally bore the subtitle, 'Poems for Alastair.' Alastair is the "you" in all of these poems. At the time that I made his acquaintance, in an online poetry discussion group, he lived on Baffin Island, employed by an Inuit organization. This flavoured some part of our early discussions, and apparently, it had a great impact upon my imagination. He has since relocated to the capital region.

Some 300+ love poems resulted from the conversation that we had, over the first years. The core of these are included in this manuscript, while a few found their way into my previous collection, *A Night for the Lady* (Ronsdale, 2013), and a few more await the light of day, seed stock for another collection.

While references to Inuit cultural property and northern references generally may stand out, there are references embedded from many indigenous nations across the landmass, from west coast to east, and I give thanks for the teaching stories, good guidance, inspirations. The story of hummingbird and heron was used with permission of Mary Fontaine, who shared it with me. Alongside these indigenous cultural references, there are other literary and song references, sometimes acknowledged within the specific works.

The bulk of the book documents an internet romance, supplemented with phone calls: the final section shares some of the poems written in response to our early in-person visits. Geographical references in the book for the most part signify places that my work brought me to, which eventually proved to be useful for meeting a friend who also travelled for work; in all cases they reflect the place that most directly inspired the poem, usually the place of writing.

My thanks to Alastair Campbell, for 'all forms of love.' While I am no longer bleeding love poetry, the conversation continues.

Joanne Arnott
10 December 2013

Biographies

JOANNE ARNOTT is a Canadian Métis/mixed-blood writer, born in Winnipeg, Manitoba, and living in Coast Salish territories on the west coast. A publishing and performing poet since the 80s, a blogger in more recent years, Joanne is mother to six young people, all born at home. Active participant in many online and inworld collaborating groups of writers, she is a mentor and piecework editor, an essayist, teacher and speaker, as well as a poet and activist. Joanne's first book, *Wiles of Girlhood*, won the Gerald Lampert Award for best first book of poetry. She is the author of *Steepy Mountain love poetry* (Kegedonce, 2004), *Mother Time* and *A Night for the Lady* (Ronsdale, 2007, 2013). *Halfling Spring: an internet romance* is Joanne's eighth book, and her sixth book of poetry.

LEO YERXA is an award-winning writer, illustrator and artist. His first book, *Last Leaf First Snowflake to Fall*, was a finalist for the Governor General's Award for Illustration and his most recent book, *Ancient Thunder*, won the Governor General's Award, and many other accolades. Leo was born on the Little Eagle Reserve in northern Ontario. He studied graphic arts at Algonquin College in Ottawa, fine arts at the University of Waterloo, and has worked with Tom Hill, a respected figure in aboriginal art in Canada. Leo was the first indigenous person in Canada to design coins for the Royal Canadian Mint incorporating indigenous design elements and First Nations athletes (Series IV 1975 Olympic Coins, Montreal Olympics 1976). A set of his murals can be seen at the Kay-Nah-Chi-Wah-Nung Historical Centre on the Rainy River First Nations National Historic Site in Ontario. Leo previously illustrated Al Hunter's first book of poetry, *Spirit Horses* (Kegedonce 2002). Leo lives in Ottawa, Ontario.